The Ones with Difficult Names

The Ones with Difficult Names

Poems by

David Brendan Hopes

Cover design by Shay Culligan

ISBN: 978-1-63980-083-4

Kelsay Books
502 South 1040 East, A-119
American Fork, Utah 84003
Kelsaybooks.com

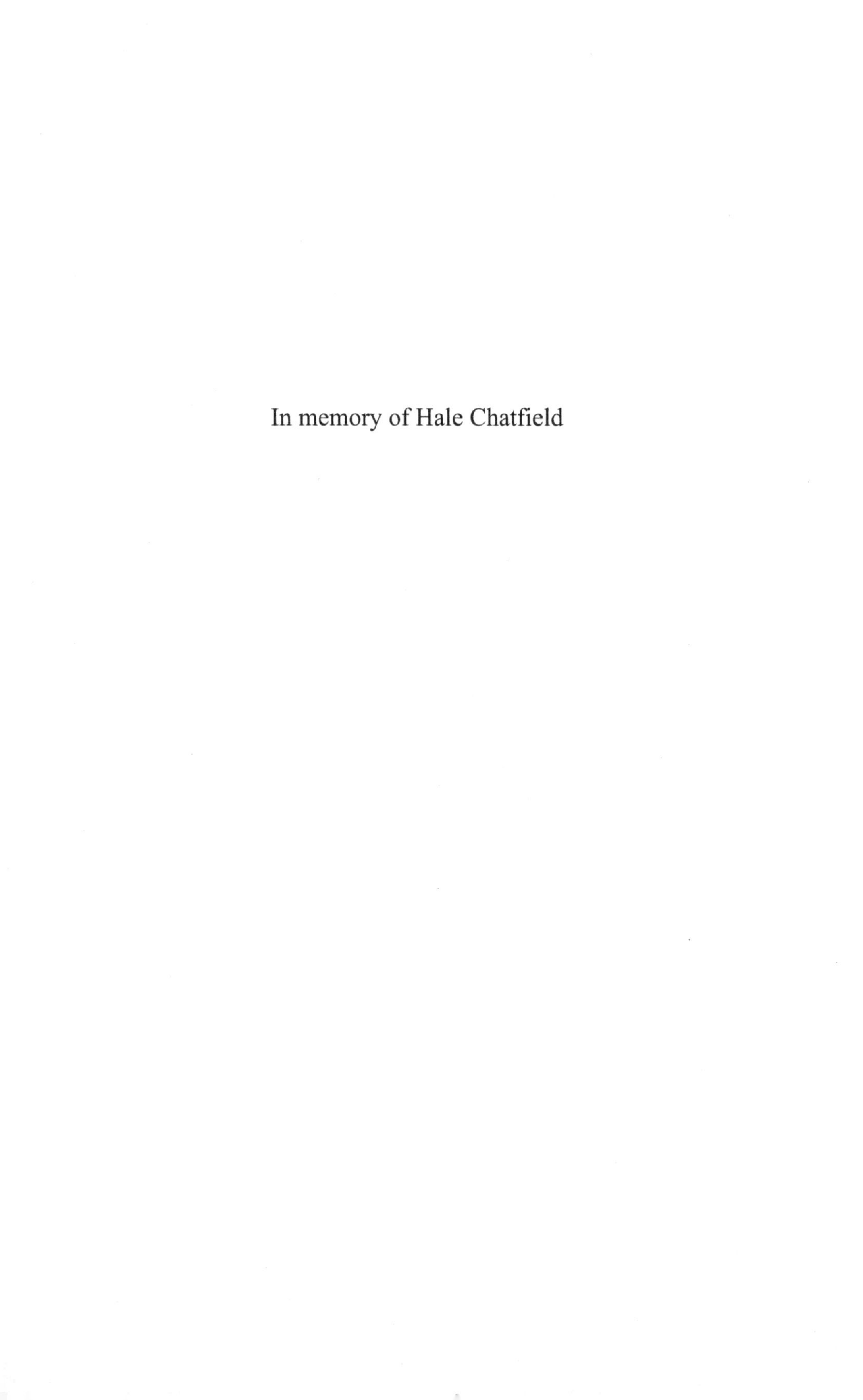

In memory of Hale Chatfield

Acknowledgments

Harbinger Asylum: “After Looking at Paintings by Samuel Palmer”

Halcyone Literary Review: “The Cuckoo”

Salt River Review: “The Ones with Difficult Names”

The Arts Journal: “The Soul May Be Compared to a Figure Walking”

Prime Number 2011: “Zen Preludes”

Contents

The Last Poet in the Poets' Café

What do they think they're doing with their heads bent
over diaries chocked with words concerning words,
the cappuccino with the white swirl atop, that this
establishment is famed for, cooling on the tabletop?
I slouch from one to the other, weeping.
Their eyes fall upon the scribbled page, thinking I weep
the lay of the last bad line. They think this is something
which can be amended by judicious revision.
They think if they put it in first person,—
attach a tag from Eliot—

the din is me howling on the patio,
banging a big drum in the cadence worst for poetry.
The ripples in the set-down coffee cease.
The bitten bagel suspends midair.
It is time for brutal honesty. Time for this age,
which never built to last, to fold its tent and go.
For God's sake close the notebook
and look at me. I am the last poet.
The last you will ever know. Can the chatter.
Pull the plugs. Put down the pens.

I am he who understands that Eisenhower,
somewhere, is forever President,
and the co-eds dress their sweater sets
with sweet sixteen birthday hearts from dad,
and Saint Francis Einstein of the Roses is moving to the suburbs,
and if you were serious you'd have spent your last dime
on a flight to Venice where you'd haunt the streets
where Pound was rumored to pass by
walking with his black cape spread and his black stick
tapping the opening dactyls of the Greeks.

Of wrath, goddess—of Peleus' son,
of Emily in her white dress, of Sylvia among the saucepans—
Anybody. Take your pick. I have already consigned
the teacher who told you, "You have a way with words;
you should be a writer," to the Circle of the Wasters of Time,
where cold waves hit the cold shore while the infinity
of the upright read their upright poems and there is no end.
If you were serious you would hunker (as one has hunkered)
in the empty classrooms, in the bar an hour before closing,
beating out rhythm, asking what words the rhythm meant.

I ruined everything, wanting this. I acknowledge it.
Now I want some just reward.
I want the beautiful boy at the next table to look at me.
I want him to forget his cappuccino till it cools.
I want the stranger to send over a drink
and for it to join the five or six other
in-honor-of-me cocktails lined up waiting to be drunk,
such as happened in the old days, pink and clear and
rich oak barrel brown, and it won't matter
I'll be good for nothing afterwards. Someone will see me home.

Someone will open the car door and whisper,
"Sir, I think this is where you live,"
and I not even wondering how he knows.
Quizzed later, he will say, "He was the last one. The wind
raged. The sleet fell. What else could I do?"
I am the last poet come among you to shout the names
which, given what I see, you will never equal.
The way is old and hard. Objectionable personalities
have taken it. The hieratic, the long-legged birds stand
by the entrance as they did, and say, still, nothing.

Poets come and poets go, but the last is the last.
Let there be some commemoration.
Let wreaths by woven from the thorns, and worn.
Let some stone be levered into place
with appropriate inscriptions upon.
Notify the Muses that one passes on his trick knee,
with his irritating manner, toward night,
and after him, for reasons already stated,
there shall be no other. Loose ribbons from bright hair.
Tear the shining garments.

A Visit to the Zoo

I

The elephants—someone blames the Carolina clay
they roll in and with which they dust their
considerable bodies—are red. Ochre, really,
such as the cave men painted them, elephant and
cave man painting the elephant red before all history.
Mrs Kramer in kindergarten gave us a gray crayon
for coloring the elephants. I will not forgive her.
Several of them have selected shade,
in which they bathe as if the shade were water,
cooling the various planes and creases.
Another has found the actual pond.
The way he hammers with his tree feet,
probes with tusk the muddy bottom,
makes one imagine he means to open up a dwelling
underneath, for when the light and air—
for reasons unclear at the moment—drift away.
Look! The pond is deeper than we thought.
Vast as he is, he has almost disappeared,
a red Atlantis heaving for a moment and then gone.
You turn to something else before he re-emerges.
You assume he will.

A neighboring elephant—the swimmer's aunt, or something—
paints with her trunk, holding the brushes,
which she selects and discards
with unmistakable discrimination.
Not this one, she says, *that* one.
The videos provide unnecessary proof.
We were waiting for this to happen.
She chooses red and yellow, but the images
are sad, turbulent. Klein-like;

they should be black and Prussian blue,
but no one has told her.
Would you think sadness and turbulence must be
the same for elephants as for men?
No matter how many bowls of fruit
and plaster casts of Venus they set before her,
she paints her inner world. The artist's red,
small eye should tell us something.

2

One woman says,
Yes, of course, Heather, the elephant
has a vagina just like everybody else.

3

The horn of the rhinoceros—
have you noticed it?—
points, as a finger on a page of text,
to the sources of the morning light.
The rhinos are mystical and impractical,
aiming their precious horns
at phenomena either too distant
or too blinding to be of immediate significance.
The rhinos sometimes
mistake themselves for kingfishers.
The result is ludicrous
and touching in almost equal measure.
We must go on, though we have
ever but imperfectly understood them
with their medicinal horns,

their delusion and dissatisfactions,
bashing the trees with their prodigious selves
until the white stars fall like flowers.

4

Your musk turtle,
common in the various native muds,
gains glory from association with exotics all about.
Lechwe drink from the edges of the turtles' lake.
Two lions differ.
A child cries "A turtle! Look!" and everyone
leans over the rail to gape as if something
wonderful had come, which might not, in this exact way,
        come again.

Another child screams
and another mob of siblings and grandparents
lean over to look.
Imagine what would happen if the rail gave,
hurling them headlong to the lake, here half waterlily,
among the turtles each as big as a helmet,
martial, enduring, with such subtlety
lying in wait.

5

The elephants are not gray and the gangly
gamine giraffes are not yellow.
The flamingos dwell in unexpected squalor.
The look on the otter's face is—disturbingly—not mirth.

The boy gorilla masturbates—knowingly, I think—
ten inches from the human ten-year-olds.
The vampires cat-lick from their bowls of blood.
The father plucks the sweaty shirt from his chest.
The squirrel daredevils in the den of ocelots,
as if rewarded for going past the line.
The pigeons fly in and out, and we hope
something inside will eat one as we watch.
We have learned something. It was worth the trip.
We saw the Amish children feeding the giraffes.
We saw the razor-y raptors clinging to their branches,
the cruel wing muscles bunched just enough
so as to take—should the door be open—
into the stark and central blue unanswerable flight.
We are the same animal we were when we arrived.
That is something, considering the rich palate
of alternatives, consider the way we itched
within our skins, wanting to be gone, to be other,
wanting anything outside this encircling cage of bone.

An Everlasting World

An everlasting world is made
of things which are themselves impermanent.

An everlasting world, the cynic may observe, is made of
lyrically mutable disappointment

converging with a singer willing to cast his lot
with such a momentary task.

But I think now of tea brewed in that old green pot
one got for nothing at a yard sale.

I think of the coned hill visible from my window,
which vulgar new construction does not quite annihilate

in its colloquy with the geese and stars.
I think of the friend I will meet in an hour, for coffee,

in the public place, where friends
look at friends over the rims of the different sized cups.

I will not speak of the poem that has him in it
as its ornament and cornerstone,

though he will know, somehow,
as all such things are obliquely known.

What should have gone forth went forth.
We live in expectancy;

we perish in fulfillment of some certain thing.
No one is so mad as not to call this a blessing.

We too into the extended fray go marching,
armed in our peculiar ways, deadly and

restorative at once, in the way we have, wasting the cities,
pulling the frightened kitten from the drainpipe,

sobbing at the innumerable gravesides sitting down
with friends over coffee, in the public place,

where we throw back our heads and laugh out loud.
Over nothing. Over catastrophe and all that.

Over some remembered bloom, sky-blue
(I'll think of the name in a minute)

Bell-shaped, nodding to the ground. You know,
the one that grandma cherished in her bit of garden,

for reasons coming clear to us: the one that grows
only after coruscating fire.

The Almost Satisfactory Lunch

The delicious, cool tea,
the chili which,
if I had not the words “hot” and “spice”
would make the tea’s figure on the tongue—
cooling and burning: one song with two refrains—
the cool-hot salad with its ooze of spice,
the altogether satisfactory lunch,
the treat to myself between two duties.
The bistro is full
(the maitre d’ wished I’d sit at the bar
to save a table, but I did not);
the fat woman watching her thin companion
select from the dessert tray;
the nephew, I guess, with his aged aunts,
looking at albums pulled from embroidered bags,
he saying the right things, they mesmerized
by his dark handsomeness; the waitresses
hovering; the bartender going a little heavy
for patrons he likes; a blur of female laughter.
I recognize, suddenly,
I am the only one alone,
at a table I had taken without thinking of this,
imagining it might not matter,
greens and chili become dust, then,
in my mouth, me waving off the refills,
the dessert tray, rising,
hurling too much money on the table,
heading to the door, as if I were dissatisfied,
as if called suddenly by something which
without me could not happen, by someone
who needed me, then, there, now,
into the noon of the parking lot, swallowing hard.

Blessing Before Sleep

Blessed be rat that skitters in the night,
be owl that breaks the rat's back,
the toothy weasel gnawing owl's bones.
Blessed be the voice I heard in blackness,
the invisible lamenter, howling the secrets of the heart.
Blessed the gut sickness, cleansing the song.
Blessed the six seeds that bound the Lady to hell.

Blessed the face at the mirror,
the one I forgot, the original,
my first face scoured and gone.
Blessed, O blessed, that this night dies.

Benediction Before Sleep

Lie down for a time, my animals,
dependable bones, forbearing feet,
graspers, bellows, quick blood
bearing me where I want to go.
My dancers and my fortresses,
let down.
All that we could move was moved.
All that could come was called home.
All that was attainable we went
the whole way seeking.
Now fold, my swans, this little time.
Look at yourself upon still water.
Arch, vault, sanctum of ribs.
Believe what soul says, lying down.
What was summoned comes,
eating the long miles in its haste.
What was sought
seeks you, as the moon does,
pared to a sickle, spending itself
in longing when you fled away.

Tokens

I think I chose wrong,
taking my symbols from the snowdrift swans,
the curved moon and the scorching crowd of stars.
Better the black cormorant with half its neck
out of black water, the ouzel
skittering the barrier between firmaments,
burning air and drowning river.

I should have chosen what scavenges for its life
at the foul seams of the world.
I should wait to see who makes it to the end.

On Those Days When I Thought Love Would Save Me

Consider those thousand valuable things which have nothing to do
with the longing of a body for a body:
fixing an appliance, or writing a poem,
or achieving those peaks on the meringue—which I despair of—
or walking an old street in an older city,
thinking those thoughts of such fragility
they disappear into the air at the honking of a horn or
whine of a panhandler from the shelter of a roof—
thoughts that might not be of bodies after all.
Cupid, finally, must be reproved
for his assumption that all bells rung
are rung for him.

For all the cunning of my words, in poems, in homilies
to the inquiring young, I have learned nothing.
Same temple, same altar heaped with blossoms,
lumbering through the manifold muds, roots in my teeth,
kicking my legs in dreams like a sleeping dog.
I cry for bodies, for the body approaching,
for the body turning away, for the memory of bodies
even at an age where such a thing's no longer fuel for poetry.
Cupid, you bastard, with your arrows
which maim but do not, it appears now, kill.
I never learn. I need once again to fight
as I did when there was none but you to tell me how.

For on those days when I thought love would save me
the furnace would be out and I'd have to wallow in the crawl space
with the unfamiliar tools in my hand, banging at the hellish thing,
making comparison, whether I would or no, between it
and the beating heart of all the world, all that stubbornness
and cold, liable to leap to flame with your hand still in it,

liable to bank its fires until you freeze and move away and
then come forth in splendor, wondering why you didn't
wait just that moment longer—
why, just that moment longer,
you didn't bet on it against
all testimony of soul and sense, and

on those days when I thought love would save me
the east in its flamingo and slate and the west
in flame of martial gold would sing the songs of work, of war,
of Mystery, of self-help with its stupid smile, of money
in the gray vault, all the songs but love, and I would
wonder if I'd come late, or to the wrong place, or all the
matter of love was closed, used up by knights and geishas
and those Hollywood types with the battlements of teeth,
and me standing there murmuring "love, dove, above"
like some Achilles with his brains knocked out,
surveying the windy plain,
no idea, anymore, of what brought him there.

On those days when I thought love would save me
I'd be startled from sleep by voices that I took for yours
whether forgiving or asking forgiveness didn't matter,
for the tone they had of *come, come,* and believe me,
I would come, to the window, to the door, the wings on my heels
stirring the dust of household neglect, and needless to say
it would be not you but some everyday thing that I would love
for a moment for your sake, an old song on an old CD,
the postman with something to sign at the door, the cats tumbling,
a branch a-scrape a window,
the nothing that becomes
the everything of distracted life.

When I think I could have been one of the heroes of love
I blame you for potential unfulfilled; I blame you
for the morbid watchfulness, the unhealthy concentration
on the motion of exterior things, the flutter of an eyelid,
the bunch of a muscle under tight cloth, the way the tongue
stays in the middle of a word, and when it finishes
the world is changed. Because of you I see it all,
in the still beauty of the morning,
after the wide eyes of the night.
I kiss in their beds the widows who think they must remember
one dream and dream it over and over: I cuddle the
ageing bachelors grieving for their cats.

And one wishes one's lamentation didn't sound
so much like Rilke, whom one had been reading,
maybe more like Whitman, a guffaw of welcome,
the arms open to receive like God's gold bear,
Yet should you summon, should the moment come upon me,
I think now, after this welter of hesitations, I think
the answer would be yes. I know you need a hero, one to go up
like Roman candles, waving his giant arms in the twilight,
oblivious to current trends, deficient in people-skills,
sacrificial, immoderate,
problematic. Glorious.
Buddy, it's me.

On those days when I thought love would never save me,
when I thought heart and soul were skew catastrophes at war,
insane Montague, blood-sucking Capulet,
in those bad seasons I was taught were all the world,
I cried to your back retreating down the moon-lashed street:
Suppose we stop this stupid war
and admit that we have always been in love,
stone-still in the doorway,

watching over each other's sleep, besotted.
Oh, you turned then,
looked back,
as though all the ages had misspoken.

O beautiful says the mountain to the gray mist coming at it
in the single hour before morning. *Beautiful*
says the shell under the gray wave breaking.
That chorus of *beauty* as the sun moves, kissing all.
Beautiful says everyone at distance, so you will not hear.
That clarity, that white beam walking before you where you walk,
the coronet of swans above, visible for miles,
the old stories you must kick away like debris
from your shoes at the door in order that we start again
must instill
a radical sense
of confidence.

They say you never forget your first love. I attest to this.
I was lost before the first half testament was written.
Out in the morning dark the first gold leaves are falling.
The hummingbirds I have fed all summer rise and drink
and take the flowers of themselves unto the flowers of the south.
It's a morning to open the bedroom windows on,
to buy on credit something to conceal the gaps, amassing,
plugging the holes, gathering that jackass fortitude we have
kept in reserve, "Force" and "Futility" written on the
knuckles of our fists, that wisdom
so like folly
God Himself must look again.

The Ones with Difficult Names

The least beetle walks like flame between the flames
of flowers.

My bitter father transforms into a sage, wrinkled and smiling.
Evening comes and children laugh upon his doorstep.

What was ash within my hand
becomes diamond with much pressing.

Night speeds with bent brave wing
between the cities and the mountain.

I think I have been writing one poem and jamming it
into one tune, and I think, after all, that has been right.

My brilliant peers have fallen by the wayside.
I with my one string and boring O of wonder have endured.

Listen. The secret was whispered me as I gathered
the worst flowers, the ones with the difficult names

and the trying habitats between the cataracts
and the blue ice,

the ones in the thoroughfares, first trampled,
hardest fighting back.

One verse and one refrain, which have,
against expectation, filled my mouth with praise.

At the Old Europe Café

1

Underneath all chaos, romance.

2

Until the epic comes, I'm making a list of
images used to keep the illusions alive
until such time as they are no longer illusions:
that way you stand in the mirror that hides the paunch,
that emphasizes the manly sweep of chest, the shoulders
which, if called upon, could uplift, could batter down,
could hammer through;
the tales you tell wherein the impossible subtleties
of life resolve into a set of rules,
masterable, a goal line you can cross
and shout, *goddammit, **there**;* the knock that comes
at midnight, and, lo, you fit the category; for you
they were looking all along.
You have the cape, the wand, the magic bracelets
it seemed nobody was going to call for,
now stirred to action, the vocabulary
of immanence cried out like song.
As the coffee hits my lip I think I should be
somewhere, doing something,
that I was meant to be . . . someone . . .

I go for cream.
I fold the book face down on the table to keep my place.
Somewhere. Something. A swirl of ivory in umber . . .
The sparrows dive around my feet, cocking their heads
to assure themselves I have no pastry,

nothing to give them, useless, worthless,
taking up space . . . .

I realize
I can make a list of my faults and blame, for
every one of them, the universe,
with perfect justice, with absolute futility,
and make of them, thereby, a somber poetry,
so to fill the record of another year.
O, I cry, keening as a *grand dame* might
somewhere between theater and heartbreak,

I am learning all this as if for the first time.
I'm running past my teachers, seizing
the banners from their hands. . .

So, I am sitting at the Old Europe Cafe.
Sparrows glean the pastry crumbs
everybody is leaving except me.
Morning coffee drinkers reassure each other
about their health, about the state of marriage—
ostentatiously not their own—how the thrice-betraying
decorator will come, certainly, today.
I flip a page. The sparrows flutter.
I'm pretending not to write a poem.
I'm pretending friendly indifference
to the inclined heads, the rattled papers,
the wrists bent in the posture of stirring,
the eyes shifted to the beauty striding
on its way elsewhere, the eyes
pretending not to notice—no two pairs
of eye-beams intertwined, as in the romances,
but seeking, seizing on a fleeting form,
easing back before they are detected.

Beneath all chaos. . . beyond romance. . .

Me, I'm pretending to have somewhere to be
in fifteen minutes, when the world starts work.
(I have a night class! See! Here is my book
with the right passages underlined, with
notes in the margin. I am serious about something!)

I'm pretending to have a mortgage
and three demanding children
from whom I have stolen a moment to write—
well, a letter to the editor, a sales strategy,
a dispassionate analysis. Surely not a poem.

The gliding beauties offer themselves.
They say, "If you would write of me
instead of the condition of your boring soul
all the time, somebody might care."
I know they are right.
I turn myself around three times.
Utter the spell.
Hold the pages down against the sudden wind

3

Executives descend at noon in clean shirts,
cloud creatures from the tossed clouds,
shining and ravenous.
The notion that they are not gods
is an accident of superficial information.
Say I transported onto Battery Park
from some oblivious antiquity.

Say one of them passes in his blaze of shirt,
his flower tie, his forest flower smell.
Would I not throw myself before him,
rash and desperate with need,
would I not ask, "Spirit, what do you require?"

If lunch, I would get him lunch.
If love, I would settle back, open the instrument case—
the golden, the little-used-of-late,
lift the instruments of love out one by one,
let the dust clear in the wind,
let the burnished facets gleam.

Underneath romance, chaos.

Now that I am on *that* track, there is no leaving.
Put away all inclination toward philosophy.
In the five big building and the three parking lots
visible from this chair I have had nine lovers.

*Who is dead, who is married, who has walked past
without acknowledging?*

Faces bend at the windows,
soft mouths, unbuttoned garments in the alley,
mysterious doors half open,
music within like a handkerchief
redolent of conflicting scents—
alluring, intimate, forbidden,
freezing your shoes to the sidewalk
so you neither enter nor rush on.

Here, a mutual touching of hands.
Here a glance across the body of this tree,
basswood, blooming then, a tabernacle of perfume.
One met here who came with me
to spite an inattentive lover.
One met here who came with me
to be reminded of what was lost.
One met here who came with no questions,
answering none, love's memory
as a flash of lightning lingers.

I came to this town to ruin my life.
I wanted to die young and beautiful like the rest.
I was not up to it.
My capacity for tragedy is, if vivid, of short lease,
and as tragedy goes, so goes glory.

Venereal shades gather round,
wondering for what they were betrayed.

We thought you were one of us.

I answer, "Gentlemen,
surviving comes as a surprise."
I tell them, "Lost spirits, pardon.
This is not the life I meant."
I keep to myself the clincher:
"I am almost content."

The Soul's Capacity to Bear Sadness

I have been exploring the soul's capacity to bear sadness.
To do this I have summoned the image of my mother
in her white nightgown, bent over,
crying in the midnight hallway, I forget why.

I have thought of my little black and white dog
who died when I was away at school,
but who came to me in a dream, and it was perfect,
and all the long-loved voices drifted out the windows,
and it was a night of blessing, of forgiveness—
then behind came the strange, dark waters
with their other voices, alluring and unfamiliar.
I tried to enter.
They tell me not to dwell on that.

Oh, be transparent, the midnight voices said,
leave nothing obscure. Leave nothing behind.

I thought of my knuckle blood reddening your door,
you on the other side listening, curious,
as though more than one thing might have happened.

I think of my poems with their goods on their backs
like refugees shambling through an unanticipated wasteland.

I think of laugher behind a closing gate.
Go ahead, one says to the heart. *Get it all out.*
This is our experiment. This is what we need to know.

It's a study which does not repay much concentration.
Looking from your vantage to the side is best.
Side eye. Left field.
Through an album of somebody else's lovers.

A touch here, a rill of fragrance,
a syllable uttered so that you must break stride.

Does the world know how much can be borne
and leave the soul the soul?
Are there records to be broken?
Does it expect growth in this arena?
Does it anticipate
some bad expansion deeper down and darker in?

The goldfish you took the trouble to name
glides amid the rocks you bothered to stack just right.
He must be blessed, you think, dwelling among
the stems of waterlilies. He eats from your hand.
He could be extinguished by the pulling of a plug.
You could do it. Once thought of, it's hard
to push it from your mind.

Described some certain way, you have to laugh
at annihilation.
You have to think of it as one of those
uncomplicated ironies even children understand.

The four-rayed starbursts of the foam flowers
throng between the porch slats. You remind yourself
they are for a day. One only. Do not get involved.
Move on.

His email says, "I love you."
It means something, even if those days are gone.
You love him back, of course. You say so and hit "Send."

You hear your own cry somewhere this side of the horizon.
You look out trying to fathom how it came to be:
the softness that makes cruelty easy—
the cruelty that makes kindliness absurd.
Maybe the hibiscus with its Sauron eye of wheeling fire.
The lads in the street, their bad vocabulary. Maybe that.

The radio in the next room plays something beautiful.
You are content to listen from a distance,
knowing that there is, essentially, no escape,
knowing you will not be able to refrain
from turning forever to the point
where the last of you went down.

In the Georgia Aquarium

The great fish in the Georgia Aquarium
go around and around, mostly—but by no means absolutely—
in the same direction, baring the architecture of flank and belly,
the white pleats, the glistening, nine-colored armor,
the patterns alternately useful and gratuitous.
Some move in schools, some in solitary majesty.
We pass under them in the reassuring posture
of the predator examining its prey.
The informative persons stationed here and there tell you
the snaggle-toothed sharks are frightening, but harmless.
The eager-eyed tarpons, the mostly-all-mouth groupers,
the bull-browed, saw-jawed and razor-ranked,
the traveling-in-packs, the lying-in-wait,
those armed for battle in the deep, are each so docile,
so in harmony they go but round and round, and children watch.
The spade-headed firmament of whale shark, the devil-headed
thunder cloud of manta-ray are gentlest of all.

(Something, I think, is not included in this picture.
Something devours in the deep.
Something is devoured. The little fish are swift.
There must be a reason.)

You can pet the rays, whose knobby skin
is such a surprise. Not all of them, though.
There must be an exam, an interview,
painstaking observation on the part of those
excelling at such things to see
who will not give the game away.

That bridal veil of poisoned lace, the jellyfish;
the white squid toothed upon its arms;
the sharks they do not have but which they must acknowledge
on the wall charts, gliding and blank-eyed, handsome,

as killers often are: I will think of these a while.
These make the whole thing fit into my hand.
The belugas—I think the captions hint at this quite broadly—
are mystical beings, neither fish nor beast,
like us only in the beauty of the bodies.
The speak with the bubble in their heads.
One hung close to the glass wall all the while, and at last,
after many attempts on her part, after I had turned away,
but turned back for reasons not quite clear, I heard her,
heard what she prophesied: *Night comes*
even here. Doors they keep hidden open.
Pools they sealed begin to seethe.
Climb, climb out, ascend, whoever can.

So Much Is Supposition

So much is supposition.

Consider me alone in the A+ downtown hotel,
drinking the excellent coffee, looking up from
time to time at the tub of orchids on the table
on the rich rug, reminding myself that I
am not hungry or in (much) pain,
wondering what the hell is wrong with me
that I should tremble at the stirring of a door,
that I should chock my chair against the wall,
eyes on all entrances, as though against an onslaught,
every face set down in memory,
license numbers recorded, details etched;
that I should check the documents the hundredth time.
That I should steam the bedroom window
with my exertions.
That I should weep.

Someone passing through to the Versailles
of the breakfast room would think,
seeing me bent above the open book,
eyes a-glitter, pen in hand,
that I am a poet hammering out
thc fatc of things, cmpathic,
majestic with disinterest.
So much, as we said, is supposition.
Let them think that.

Really,
we have had the worst day, and after that, one worse.
Give us a sandwich, a cocktail, an hour to catch our breath.

Gun-shy and quivering,
I lie in wait–that is the fact behind it all—
ready to move on when the answer "yes" to any question
shall mean "yes," when the door opened
shall be opened from the other side
and the salutation is "come in. "

When the ensuing day will not deliver us back to "start,"
the hard-won ground will not revert to the enemy while we sleep,
when the dreadful whirling on the maps shall not delay
and we shall be home before the airports close.

So much is supposition.
So much time spent underlining the significant verses,
memorizing those potent to push us to another dispensation.

        If the line be but perfect—
        If the image cut to the fire's heart—

(Handsome waiter asks if I need my cocktail freshened.
By all the gods of thunder, yes.)

Let the spirits who received our reason and our pleading
on the darkest of all nights hover over.
Allow them patience. Let us state our case.

This mood irks everybody.
I'll move on from it
when an army of lovers shall not fail,

when after mortal expenditure something is marked "paid,"
when Order shuts up when its point is proven,
when the broken are allowed a moment to recover,
when Reason has the last sweet say.

If you think I'm making poetry,
I have a thing or two to show you.

I but make ready:
that the child of the Actual and the Ideal pass
in clouds of floating frankincense before us—
that all things do not need to be well, but only one or two—
that when you kneel wounded in the snow
and let your blood sink through,
there will grow, in some season not yet present to the mind,
a rose, or an orchid, or a bee with see-through wings,
something stronger, for that red rain, than it meant to be.

Have crackers and charcuterie ready for the long haul.
Run a tab.

Let someone write this down "acceptable."
Let someone write this down "enough."

The Cuckoo

Cuckoo recommends herself to certain souls
by reason of her homelife, which is none.
Lays her eggs in others' nests—famous for it—
confident that her lummox progeny
will triumph over whatever wren or finch
was intended as the true inheritor.
(The happy-go-lucky male lacks even this
responsibility. He fucks and flies and is,
therefore, a god.)

Europe forgives him for his music.
Cuckoo knows to open the air to beneficial discourse,
for what goes out as music must come in, elsewhere,
as wisdom.

Cuckoo stands, then, for enlightenment:
for he is free;
for he devours the noisome things
that otherwise would gnaw the forest bare;
for he is innocent of the heaviness of other lives,
and thus marks in purity
the ways of the Wood to Come.
The first road is the best road until it is not,
and then it is again.

Cuckoo. . . Cuckoo. . . sounds stupid
only when the stupid say it.

Serious commentators wonder why the gods love
a soul so feckless.
I can't find the answer they were looking for.

Cuckoo woke me as I slept upon a stone
in Connemara, and for twelve months I was blessed.

Cuckoo cried in the sassafras above my head.
Flee the coming wrath, he told me. I did not look back.

Cuckoo called in the elderberry thicket. I dug there,
found the treasure. Left it lie.

We have the black billed and the yellow billed.
Know them apart by the varied silence left behind.

The cuckoo who has learned what he
must say to earn his morning meal cries out:

> *For seven days refrain*
> *from that which makes you beautiful.*
> *For seven days meditate upon the caterpillar.*
> *Then return to me.*

Seven days upon the caterpillar being hard,
few return.

The gods bestow their blessings,
cuckoo having recommend himself to them
by reason of things that were not his doing,
by dint of spending nothing,
pausing for nothing, cashing in where he had not invested.

Strange the praise in heaven for this.
It's not what you expect.
The bodhisattvas all sigh "Blessed!"
to the glade where the cuckoo called,
longing, paradoxically, to obtain, enclose,
to be enshrined in his sharp heart forever.

Peace-in-the-Valley

I want a name for the spirit that is with me
in the blaze of this September morning, after the blue moon
of a yellow August, while hurricanes churn
through the gunmetal sea and swallowtails
fray at the edge with too much life.

I think it is the Spirit of Politics.
I will leave God alone just now
for her blessings, select, austere, almost enough.
This is the Spirit which arrives
after fury and before beginning again.
Modest, in poets not the liar she is in the world.
The one who prepares. The one who would change
her white gown to scarlet at a whisper of invitation.

It is the Spirit of my 30s going to sleep.
Oh, I am forty. I am forty and five minutes.
I am forty and an hour. I hold my face
in that gesture which is hilarity and despair.

        Spirit is a body dancing.
Changed from that airiness into steel.
Changed from that airiness into granite and diamond.
Changed from possibility into strength,
digging root into the passages of the world.
Change almost well.
Change almost to be sung.

        (Over the rooftops,
        across the wide valley,
        I see the mountains grown so light.
        I see the mountains leaping, gathering their skirts,
                shaking their gold bangles the sycamores,

shaking their red bangles the maples,
shaking dark bangles,
beating their black knees.

I say to the spirit which is dancing in the mountains,
I say to the spirit,
I say, O dance with me!)

Perhaps it is the Spirit of Peace,
white lotus in my pool of crocodiles.
He comes with purity around him shimmering,
in cloth-of-moonlight, beautiful and hopeless,
dumfounded with the knowledge
I will never, in this life,
love him.

Perhaps, as ever, the Spirit of Defiance.
I tell him, "Teach me," and he begins the old sweet song.
He remembers for me Sarah's laughter,
Nimrod's crown and tower, the Hebrews' tricks
before the throne of Pharaoh,
the feet of Moloch held to the prophetic fire,
the fig tree withered by the tantrum of a god.
He tells me of the ways beside, the ways around.
He sings me of that Aepyornis
who with his gut-kick brought down elephants,
hummingbird's cousin daring immensity to war.

He rumors to me of gifts and dispensations,
loves, dreams, visions—of men whose hearts
tied God's in love-knot and went forth,
the white rose springing from their wasted blood.

He tells how we were led by insubstantial voices
generation upon generation dying in the wilderness,
and how we have forgiven everything.

Perhaps he is just the Spirit of the Flower,
that white vine spread beneath my window by its own will.
My neighbor calls it peace-in-the-valley.
By night it's heart's-purple,
a lavaliere of judging eyes,
Behemoth's footprint planted in my lawn.
    I say he is a rebel's nosegay. Star-shaped. Evergreen.
    Peace-in-the-valley to repent;
    Peace-in-the-valley to repay:
    flower's Body for the fear that forced me,
    flower's Spirit for love that lay down long ago.

      Listen, I say leaning back with my lips
      to the flowers' ear, *what I sing you.*
      It is better now than what was given.
      It is better now than what I am.

"Beautiful," You Say to the Mirror

You begin the day by asking the cats if your socks match.
You begin the day by dabbing on the various
emollients and preventatives,
choosing the garments that here conceal and here reveal.
You begin the day by fighting back the dreams
        that come before waking,
        in which you lead the scattered peoples home,
        in which you fly to the manifold rescues—
the ones where you are
what you planned to be when—tow-headed, elbow-bruised—
        you first thought of being anything at all.

You begin the day anxious to assert such milestones
as are yet clearly marked, touchstones easy of access,
        so even the stupid and the
        willful enter sanctuary before full night.
You arise hoping to affirm the paradigms reign
        as they reigned
        when you first awoke and found them,
        most unexpectedly, most profoundly,
                beautiful.

O then *Beautiful!* you say to the mirror, trying to remember
what that meant and what it had to do with you.
You stand at the surf's edge, calling
You ransack poems to find a word for what you feel.
You hum the themes of the noble last quartets.
There's an hour before you need
apply yourself to anything of this world.
You recognize it.
        Yes, the dead know something we do not.
        If only you yourself were dead you might just tell.

You unfold your hand
matted with blood and petals,
and make that dancer's gesture,
        the one that means
        the lost beauty is not lost, you fool.
It is a face
by a sable veil concealed, sometimes revealed,
the dancer's motions
misinterpreted by distance and the common folly of all men
so to assume it is the veil alone that's real.
Oh, if you were dead as they, you would know it all.

As it is, you're not quite sure. The face in the mirror
tries to smooth a wrinkle by holding its mouth just so.
        The body in the mirror
        swerves to the closet, chooses its disguise, then
        toward the door, planning its eager day,
exhausted, almost, with anticipation,
exalted, almost, as if it had not taken, even yet
        its first too-eager full step
                down.

Invitation to the End of History

I got the tickets on the web page which claims
you can never, therein, be disappointed.
I made reservations even though it was not, they said,
strictly necessary, in the restaurant whose cuisine
none of us fully understands.
I've warned the maitre d' to watch for you
in the unlikely case that I do not arrive first.
The walk is swept. The ways are marked.
Nothing is obscure, nothing is ambiguous
for thirty yards in every direction.
I've placed my watchmen in the wild hills
so there is no fear of being surprised.
The coast guards tend their driftwood campfires
The current buzzes in the shocking fence
that rings and buffers, heart-shaped, the perimeter.

I intend to dazzle you.
I intend to speak in those abbreviated debutante gasps
you must lean in and listen for.
I plan to leave you reeling from the shock
of so much damage done with these small bones
and this bad attitude,
so many songs howled beneath your window
with just this voice and this array of broken instruments.
I shall be a wild cat of the forest
whose voice freezes the blood
without ever making clear what he intends.
I hope you'll be impressed
by the outpouring of bravura
not much in itself but plenty for these beaten times.
My arrogant poems fall to the dust around.
My anxious fingers hurry hyacinths into flower.
This is what I set before you,
hopeful as a small boy Christmas morning.

I don't even wait for others to roar derision.
I beat them to it, the mocking face in the mirror
combing through its tangle of hair, hoping for the best.
Look, I am mad to hold you.
I shall be covert only enough
not to be dragged down every moment
by peals of ironic laughter.

I admit I have not understood one blessed thing.
I can make you a song of my repetitious failures.
I can make you a song of that man
trying to reach the moon with a ladder
of ever-magnifying size, who keeps falling back and
falling back, yet finds himself,
in an hour of exhausted introspection
possessed of a ladder most surpassing—
if not quite up to what he wanted—
high enough to overlook all things of this world.

Be assured I'm not without my allies.
Whenever I'm tempted to let
love and poetry go their way without me
into the crowd of those
for whom they were clearly meant,
Great-grandmother comes with her edged flint by the fire,
clanging her necklace of shells, scraping the red meat.
"What do you know of it?" she says.
Her hand gestures to the moon over the far snows.
One shrugs. One turns. One breathes. Moves forward.

You whom I invited out for coffee were not expecting
the dance, the acrobatics:
that vague lifting of my hand toward the bright
that is *amen,*

the silence that goes on so long
as to make everyone uncomfortable
that is praise,
the twist of my wrist toward the impenetrable dark
that is the opening of a door
through which you must both enter and depart.

(Bells around my ankles,
little fire sticks rolling on my thumbs)

I don't know what they told you
at the mysterious portal where our lives began.
I was assured that if I said the right thing
I'd be answered. Eventually.
That pretty much explains it.
The sea cries endlessly her castaways:
I do not yet hear my name among them
Therefore do I rise up.
Therefore do I sing,
in the walled garden, in the valley of dry bones.

I'm grateful you're still listening.
All that smiting of the waters,
all the skeletons and blooded banners
and the trumpets bent with victory
seem not to have driven you away.
Come lay your head against me and
I will cry no further cry,
all spears thrown
all arrows flown.
all the big kingdoms
hounded down into the dust.

I’m the one who planted you a garden long ago.
See where I come now bearing its first lily.

The Alphabet Song

The jay was dead and she gave me a box to bury him.
Find a few flowers. Toss them in.
Assume a soul where nobody has said otherwise.
Sing, as a child does
that old tune

(I'm sorry if you expected something else)

A for the alley of lilacs.
Each time a surprise—
She in the alley of lilacs,
a book of poems in her hand

a book of verses open in her hand
lilac petals
littering the page,
a shoebox for the eternity of the birds

For the apple of the orchard.
For annunciation. Annihilation.

A is for that Aepyornis
who with his gut-kick brings down elephants.

B for the bird that passes and returns.
Each time
bunting
bullfinch
age after age
Are you thinking between the lines?
Accepting the witness of the spaces?

The audacity of the open pages
the whiteness of them
as of snow unfallen
as of the egg unbroken
and yet sending forth its chick.
Imagine this. Encompass this.

C for gold Capella risen precisely between the roofs.
Cobalt. Carmine.
Cries of birds that do not live here anymore.

D for the dim, for the dead, for every dad,
for Dunkleosteus agape in the deep
outside the bedroom window

E, I think,
is everlasting. Into the East, again, again.
Who knows why?

Are you getting this?

Are you getting this down?

Are you getting this, all of it, down?

It's not that I've not repeated it enough.
It's not that I've left anything to chance.

Unbidden
Uncorrected
Striking out no single line

repenting not
considering not
hesitating not
looking neither
to the right nor to the left
brat and hero
depending on how one looks at things

E for the egret which was the last god
visible upon the water.

F is for finish like wind in the night approaching
F for the voice of silk over stone
Flight away from anywhere, to anywhere,
the dark shores closing in.

Night with its single syllable
Owl on the oak branch, wild lamenting
whom, you wonder. How could he love so many?

G is for the gold spring, golden autumn
the gold cup of my open hand.
They say to come with empty pockets
They say to come with empty begging bowl
        Oh, I have come
        sublime
        in emptiness
        singular in want
        holding out
        extending
        every vacancy
        to be filled

When I sat down in the lamplight the air said,
"I do not think you should sing of this.
"I do not think this is given to you or anyone to sing
"Go back to what you did before.
"I think
"to this point
"you have piled matter upon matter
"and done no harm
"But now,
"one flame will come and burn it all away."

Nevertheless

Bring the one flame. Bear it all away.

H is the breath, the madman said.
The exhalation
that giveth soul back into the wind
God's dying breath, the sidereal panoply
which some ears cannot hear
For it is spirit
and we are not
for it is *then*
and we are not

Dew comes to the wind and the world is made.

I comes to separate me from all that.
I.I.I.
I do what is allowed
I wear that dissatisfied face,

wear what's-his-name's mantle
that stinks so after all these years
I look to the sky and wonder
when the rains come
are there no bodies to stop
to stop the rain,
wall, shirt, window, coat, or door—
no forfending being
the rain will find a way in.
Stone, brass, steel
the rain will find a way.

I dance the crane's dance. Nobody is fooled.

I must have misunderstood
what Spirit meant
when it said, "I am with you always."
it must have been my fault in some way
a footnote overlooked
a codicil ignored
Patient night tires of that syllable "I"
Which opens every lamentation.

J is for joke.
For the one whose name will not be spoken in this mood.

K is for king
the rose and the flame entwined
for crown,
the seal and the white shark caught midair
in those nature films
devouring and devoured

the bluegill in the pickerel's pool
the waters drawing backward
air bent to let destruction pass
that is the king and his crown
that is the glory of his moving
that is the secret of his standing still

L is the lullaby
Lullay, lullay, my little tiny child.
Grandma gave me a box to put the dead jay in.
(I have turned from that, return to it now)
    To bury him.
    To put him away.
    That it might be—
    That it might be remembered—
    That the hard door might be swung—
    That it might be set in crystal
    The body and the body of fire entwined—

M turns out to be all I know,
all that can be known
given this boy bewildered
and wandering the path
his feet were set on long ago.
N is not and never.
Stop in the middle. Look both ways.
In case you wondered.
In case you financed argosies to discover
what it was.

O

That was the secret.
That was the secret of my going out.
That was the secret of my standing still.

Seven Zen Preludes: Halloween Morning: Times Square

1

This is the corner where the tourists stand
to have their photo taken
before the greatest possible concentration
of bazillion kilowatt billboards.

I'm surprised to feel so tenderhearted toward them.

They will think when they look at the picture later,
"My friend took this.
That was the day we had raw salmon.
That was the day we got the last seats at the matinee."

That it is Times Square is irrelevant.
It might as well be
Iguazu Falls
or a stand of trees
weighed down with autumn.

Oh. I wish I were taking somebody's picture,
kneeling, ignoring the crowd
to get a better angle.

2

The pigeons note my pigeon-disgusting chai, move on.
The brown sparrows come after,
perching on the rim of my table.
They're sure I've something hidden,
something kept from the complacent pigeons,

but that I may yield to them. The brown of their feathers
is more complicated than one expects.
I rise. Go to the Starbucks. Buy a bagel.
Crumble it pieces and present it to the sparrows,
bit by bit. You can tell by the casualness of receipt
this is what they expected all along.

3

A tiny Japanese girl with her face made up
to be a kitten offers me a plastic pumpkin
to put something into.
Her parents watch, beaming.
They have got the custom slightly wrong.

I have nothing. I have a plastic bottle of antacids.
I put that in.
The girl-kitten dances for joy.
The smiling parents bow, and bow.

4

The woman with the cigarette catches me
cleaning my glasses with a dollar bill.
"I learned that from my father," I say.

Tears course down the lenses,
and I have to take the dollar out again.

5

The domes I cover myself with
are the color of the air, therefore invisible.
But I know they rise above those towers
and seal the square, the city, the gray Hudson
flowing down, against whatever danger
I was sent here to prevent.

Who knew that they enclosed so much?

6
The policeman and his horse
pose for photographs.
The horse is beautiful and allows
on his nose the caress of children.

Some life in this city will be saved
by a caress on the muzzle of a beautiful horse.
The cop and the horse chant
from their quarter of the well of light

O come, O come

7

I'm sitting here weeping in gratitude
for the gift of poetry.
Passers-by think I have lost someone
and the news has just come.

Lent

I will take this hour of this day to practice writing in a hand
not only legible but gracious, my own being a tribulation
to all who read of it, a gateway of misunderstanding.

I'll test to see if the limb to which I have climbed
is really the loftiest in the forest. I will re-examine my
conviction of infallibility. I'll laugh at other people's jokes.

I will not tense when asked for the fifteenth explanation
of the same plain thing, nor shall I turn my head to mock,
like some hyena of the Jesuits, at the innocent—

if oft repeated, gong-like and deadening—misconception
of the those set in my path by—I admit it—that wise
Power dealing Patience as the summer rain deals roses.

And I think I was mistaken to consider such issues to be
trivial. I will return calls promptly. I will not let
mail climb the office wall until, like a great chasm

in the shaking of the earth, it falls, convulsing, to the
subjugated plain. Remember whose inquiries, hopes,
perhaps desires, lie amid the rubble. Ration indignation.

For the new year comes, and one may not forever
shield with personal attractiveness one's shortcomings.
That probably flickered out before I thought it did.

For I beheld me yesterday in a restaurant window,
stopped by the local crazy, she not even begging, or merely
for a moment for a listening ear,

a moment to be somebody listen to. How I contrived
to get away, squirming that squirm, lying those lies,
that look upon my face, the stiffening of my

shoulders, that mask of the demigod for an interval
disdaining to blast the irritant away, that Pharisee slump,
the corners of the lips bowed like a weapon drawn:

all as though for an audience—a choir
of angels watching, I suppose, new frontiers
of superciliousness approached and crossed.

And the Angel who is my Angel whispered,
What if Shakespeare caught you doing that?
What fool would he make you in what sly play, brayed at,

stumbling, by his lofted nose made unaware, into
the pig sties and the ox shit, the audience wishing, merrily,
he might be ground down in it, wailing in the red flare

of self-discovery, in the 5th Act, when everyone else is married?
Milton hurls you headlong into the Slough of the Prissy, not even
strong enough for hell.

What if Blake should grab your shirt sleeve in the street,
stopping you mid-sneer, while overhead
openeth the portal and the whirling spheres pour out,

the chimney sweeps and phantoms crying at your stiff back
*as they cried **Shame!** at Nobodaddy and White Jehovah in*
the worlds before?

Today I might buy a crazed old woman tea and listen.
I might shut about my standards.
I might, in some alley where nobody like me

ever goes, under a fire-escape, against the black bricks,
I might sit down amid the oil pools and wine bottles,
I might squat down with my fist in my teeth,

might squat like an animal and howl.

In the River Cherwell

In the River Cherwell
the moorhen and the moorcock and their five
soot-ball chicks pad upon the waterlilies,
the white waterlilies and the pink.

The moorcock warns away the too-close geese.
The moorhen teaches her chicks "light"
and "cool" and "waterlily" in their bell-like,
untranslatable tongue.

A black dog sleeps beside the water.

*

The black dog wakes, plunges, swims.
Ripples raise the waterlilies, slam them down.
The moorhen and the moorcock
and the five dark chicks disappear
as though they never were.

I could wait it out, this emptiness,
but that I know how it all must end.

*

The land from the ordered water must seem chaos,
its people like bewildered giants
casting to and fro on their long legs,
shouting, sitting, running, taking out their books,
putting their books away,
spreading their preposterous luncheons.

Unlike the moorhens,
there was no one
to tell them what to do.
Some struggle to abide and some to go.
Some rush to the spot from which others rush away.
I take a deep breath, try to step aside.
I sleep in the long grass, and the finger of dreams
points at the spot in the river where the sun,
at noon, rests for a moment perfect
on the soundless bottom.

*

I paddle until my feet no longer find the bottom.
Someone call me; I'll come home.

The Hour of Silent Women

. . .in the health club pool. . .

The woman who had been swimming
with rhythmic, even strokes stopped.
She stands at the shallow end with her
forehead pressed against the pool wall.
The water around her settles, quiet
as wrecks must be at the bottom.
The woman in the whirlpool with me
goes also silent, facing away
as if I were a profanation,
her freckled old shoulder, like a bird's,
at once fearful and threatening,
the harsh claws hidden by the foam.
I watch. Wait. They do not move.

Whoever they left to guard the door
failed. I stumbled unaware
into the sanctuary with my blue trunks
and my flapping feet. I called greeting
before realizing I'd come
at the hour of silent women.
The air around us bows as if
filled with that to which they must
and simultaneously cannot give utterance.
Something uses their still
limbs to climb up from places
deeper than the gym pool.
Something shakes in the deep
before it breaks into the common air. I wrap
my towel around my shoulders, leave,
not looking back, that they might
hurl their maledictions
into the hours left
before full light.

YMCA: Six Preludes in the Morning Dark

1

Because I'm a poet, everything reminds me of something
it is not, quite.
This morning's hard small moon, for instance, stood,
at the moment I regarded it, for the heart,
generous at the portals, round and golden at the horizons
of the beginning and the end, but tight gathered to itself
for the long trek through the only intermittently starry darkness.
You have a minute now to study the sky.

You go to the gym at the usual hour. Allow
the streetlights to tell you where to park so you won't
slip on black ice the first thing.
The workout clothes lie frozen in the bag,
lest one imagine for a moment things might be
easier than they're meant to be. You put them on.
You wait for the trembling to subside.

2

At the YMCA they array small tables and chairs
for a tete-a-tete, or the signing of those
documents that the meaty businessmen
bring with them everywhere,
or for a poet to spread work on for an hour.
Nobody uses them. I will. I do so while the moon
I criticize for distance and perfection
–both metaphysical affronts–
hurries to make his circuit ere the sun comes.

Increased my weights today. The burn had
sweetness to it. . . difficult to describe. . .

but like the scorching on the cheek when your lover
watches and you do not yet know,
like the chill when your lover has turned aside
and you do not yet know.

3

You believe the ease of the swimmers is a deception.
You think there must be more valor involved
in breasting away an element so inimical to life.
They submerge and emerge with equal ottery insouciance.
You yourself have never mastered the art
of keeping the head down, of facing the bottom,
trusting it will suffer you to rise again.
Some of them breathe once the whole length of the pool.
Not you. You are one who makes the air
confirm its good intentions second by second.
You will never be one of them at ease at the boundaries,
crossing and recrossing the dangerous passages,
facing the deep as though it were all one
whether one achieves that far white wall or not.

4

The swimmers suggest clouds or bleach-white waterbirds
propelled by strokes that scarcely seem sufficient—
all the blue, massy and resistant,
pushing it behind, welcoming it from before,
elementals breathing water,
taking advantage of the time between night and day,
when physics are suspended
and all the rules are the rules of dreamers.

Whither, O splendid ones,
through straits the color of the sky?
Deep chested naiads crossing from Cos to Melos
in days before the count began, sea-daughters
whom one had heard singing once at the
meeting place of waters,
grant that my head be lifted from the page
when you rise and take the shape of women,
when you walk
from pool to locker room a little unsteady
upon those unaccustomed feet,
under your gray hair singing of the tameless waters..

5

To Siddhartha, While Going to the Gym

It's so early even the traffic lights are dim.
The midnight hunters slink home fed.
Parking is easy. Those provided for
are just now tumbling out of bed.
I watch him hang his office shirt
on the peg provided by the gym.
I do not always work out at this hour,
but when I do it's because of him.
He firms the hanger, rubs the creases flat,
seems not to notice where he goes I go.
We speak. *The weather's this; our team is that.*
Do you know the restaurant I know?
When he's out on the weight room floor
I gather the white shirt to my face.

One gesture, I whisper, *one syllable*
might quench the fire. . .a brief embrace. . .
Here is another way to look at it:
the origin of suffering is denial.
To deny is to necessitate.
Let that sink in. Let that resonate.

6

I'm better in exercise class
than people expect me to be—
graceless and strong, an old bear
dancing on his hind feet.

They have those steps where you go up and down
and turn in your step while you go,
and if you give it no thought whatever
you end up facing the way you were meant to.

"Let this be a lesson to me" I think
as I fancy-foot with the nimble girls,
with the boys who are—this is the best—
watching me from the corners to see how it's done.

After Looking at Paintings by Samuel Palmer

Towered city, haunted stream. Confusion and darkness between.
This is exactly the kind of thing that appeals.

I live in the towered city among winged things
chanting and exultant.
Above sail the ten stars that whisper their secrets
and the ten that are silent until the end.
You live by the haunted stream and can sing
the wonders of ambiguity as I cannot.
All would be well if you did not call me, sometimes, down.
That oaf of moon, that yeoman lad of moon
holding darkness in his hands like
a workman's tool straitens, planes, smooths
the inconsistencies, and the path from the towered city
and the path from the haunted stream
are one, and lit by moon, and it is possible,
once, to trace where they are going.

On those nights when you
from the haunted stream and I from the towered city
wander forth under the bent and sidewise constellations,
there is such sweetness.
The bee in her domicile of honey.
The white bear sleeping in a cave of pearl,
dancers in a dark fire turning but never departing.

Palmer would paint us then, two figures in a field,
silver and shadow, or one figure
built of what were two an hour before.
There are wings we will not, presently, unfurl.
There are thrones we need not sit upon.
There are crowns but we need not wear them.
But we must at last arise and go,

must turn to towered city, to haunted stream
before morning,
holding each some token scented of the other.

No one will know. No one watched us heading out
from haunted battlements that for a night were home.
No one will see us drag back fleeing what was certain.
Perhaps they will honor our career of seeking—futilely
but with uncharacteristic resolve—
that still mysterious point,
the garden with the axle-tree,
bearing its flowers and fruits in a single hour,
perfumed with the vapor of things crushed—
None to see us reach.
None to see us, in the final possible moment, eat.

I Think of My Lover Lying Down

I think of my lover lying down
in the room of last things,
the one lit by the vase of roses. I know
he shall rise in wisdom while I'm
down in the muck with the others,
crying our ignorant maledictions.

I laid a carpet for him, intricate in weaving
its reds and ochres, the gold flash,
the crossing and re-crossing of its ways.
When he treads upon it he treads the complexity.
When lies down and lifts his feet,
what is left behind is left behind.

I unrolled the carpet and he made it a road.
I inlaid the headboard with sapphire,
for that stone gives sleep.
I surrounded the sapphire with rings of pearl,
for the making and unmaking of the water
is never at an end.

The coverlet is umber, that his bones might
feel at home under the earth.
The lamp at his bedside is like the moon,
for even in the dark it watches.
I think of what my beloved
might be dreaming

I do not ask.
If it's not of me I would despair.
If it is of me I would despair.

I think of my beloved lying down,
watching without entering,
guarding the door when the only danger lies within.

My book lies open in the lamplight.
One page only has been written.
I think of my lover waking in the room
lit by its snowstorm roses. I've tried to rig it
so he wakes in whiteness,
in whiteness read the as yet unwritten page.

Beside the River

If you've seen no other river, this one is wide.
Its half-defeated trees lean over to gaze
upon themselves. One flood tilted them.
One will fell them, float them to the Gulf under moonlight,
when, so far as this world knows, they are no more.

A trick of light makes the dazzled wavelets
seem to come ashore, as the sea does, over and over.
Mark the river switch back north
to join the Indian rivers with their luxury of names.
It goes two ways at once. This time you get to choose.

One man fishes from a failing tree.
His shirt is dirty where he cleans his hands with it.
He's too jumpy for the fat fish he's stuck with here.
He beats the water to detach the bait
and high boots it to a better spot, nearer me.

I want him to come and put his hand against my chest
that I might be assured I am alive. I do not know
exactly how to convey this desire across the little
cove of spinning leaves and carcasses. All waters
quicken, and the kingfisher on the far side screeches

as can only blood and air. The fisherman has caught
nothing the whole time I have watched.
The fish in the river quicken and come to the bait
or they do not. You can jerk the line at the right moment,
but bright eyes in the drop-offs, they decide.

I think he should drop the pole and take his cock in his hand.
He should raise it up to me as things are offered
in the wilderness, on an impulse, with no memory or return.

The fish aren't biting anyway. Or he might mosey
upstream tree by tree as he had been doing

before I came. He was seeking something. Not fish.
I wait for him, like those gods in the stories, to set fire
to the shrubbery. I wait as one is taught to do
for sudden wings, the unworldly cry, by which
one finds oneself the midpoint of some necessary story.

I wait for the crossing of destiny with destiny
until such moment as scent from a T-shirt,
an unambiguous placement of black boot,
turns me back onto the broad way I was going,
before the insinuating river whispered me aside.

In the Garden of the Barberinis

A red cat conceals among the hedges,
leaping when a bird comes close enough,
settling back upon his fire-colored haunches.
If you circle you catch glimpses of him,
a lion in reduction amid
the paradise in reduction
that is the garden of the dead princes.

Like all profound things, the cat, the garden,
the harmonious blackbird on the shattered wall,
are awake and asleep at the same time.

In the Garden of the Barberinis
it rains and it does not rain,
recovers and prepares. One looks for confirmation
of every certain thing.
The roses cannot tell you if they blush or fade.
The sky is gray damask.
Unrippled, the fountain's face. The cat
narrows his eyes as against some tempest slanting down.

The garden drinks the rain,
drinks what it knows is yet to come,
drinks what is remembered from a history of fulfilment.
The cat settles down with the fowl that once did,
but has not yet, wandered into range.
O the rose sighs, nestled in some bosom
six hundred summers in the ground.

Let me find someone to ask to stay here for a while.
I'll study with the cat, the rose, the untroubled fountain
how to be in the rain of love
and yet be waiting for it,

divining it from far off approach on obscure wings,
as such beings do that move without moving.

Let me abide.
Let me approach with unseemly speed, arms open.
Let me feel you brace for contact.
Then gaze at your receding back,
distant as another planet's moon,
knowing what will come again,
what will be approached and held despite dividing distance–
what rose and ruby and white rain
when all this penalty of time is paid.

Swan

1

Swan, unlike the rest of us,
proceeds oblivious of his admirers
upon the half-serene, half-agitated lake
all roofed with twinkling fires.

His motionless motions make
ellipses before him, and, lengthening behind,
require the argumentative waters take
a turn toward silence, to be blue, and still.

An ode to this bird among the birds, requires
a novel grammar, a rhetoric of watchfulness,
a further inclination than one had
to hold to the heart, to crave, to bless.

I can't think what in my orisons to demand,
having this wild god take bread crusts from my hand.

2

For the swan loves once
then goes his winding road alone.
He takes the further way
until the nearer way is shown.

Upon and in and on and over and amid,
swan in a blizzard of prepositions changing
status with the merest rearranging
of a snow-white wing. What I did

was watch him from the margin of the mere.
O, Ornithology!, one cries.
One believes this is the year
one lifts what one loves from the dirt into the skies.

Words vanish in the lake like summer rain.
Swan and the gleam of him afloat remain.

3

I think before this urgent day is ended
all will have spread white wing and taken flight.
All pale and dark will have been blended
into the undifferentiated blank of autumn night.

Gray has eaten up the arching blue.
The moon sleeps. The sun is blind.
It's too much to say "I go with you,"
too little to sigh "I stay behind."

I have cried now how many embarrassing times
to the bird-shape blazing on the darkened lake,
begging to be with him as he climbs.
I'm ready, almost, to forsake

what I've gathered close and sworn upon,
to take his dark road westward toward dawn.
May wingbeats make the winds to blow.
May going give the strength to go.

The Soul May Be Compared to a Figure Walking

In the forms' bare spaces they ask my occupation.
I'm tempted to tell the truth for once, tempted to write,
"I am one who finds similitudes for soul."
Yeats reports that some moralist or mythological poet
compares the solitary soul to a swan.
Heaney suggests "the soul may be compared
unto a spoonbait that a child discovers
beneath the sliding lid of a pencil case,
glimpsed once and imagined for a lifetime."
Yes. I write these out for confirmation.

The soul may be compared to a figure walking
Bent Creek Road southward from the Parkway.
Two miles down a dirt road, barred, leaps to the right.
He climbs the barricade. Takes the offshoot,
hoping it too is forbidden.
A blunt wood closes in, trees compact, in-gathered
as if to counsel reticence in that rage of space and air.
One tall tree guards the road's end, in Park Service red
warning no vehicles, no camping.
The figure neither drives nor camps.

Beyond the cherub tree a high meadow opens,
gold under the sky, grass beaten gold by wind.
A meadow with its studded carpet tilts
toward the mountains lying many-figured:
Crag, Fang, Wall, the sleeping Dinosaur, great
Pisgah in the distance like a blue bride, veiled and terrible.
Above, the bowl of air is perfect quiet.
The swallows cross and cross, and then are quiet
Lie down the voice says. *Lie amid gold and sleep.*
The figure listens and obeys.

The soul may be compared to a sleeper
on a burnished slope above which certain spirits
in the shape of birds cross and recross,
cruciform and holy, watching and being watched,
revealing those losses one is acquainted with already,
but with different names, in slightly altered stories,
so that the sorrow one put to one side days ago
announces itself again. One might bow one's head and weep.
One might start again, exerting late-learned,
sweetly dishonest magic on the middle and the end.

I think I'm saved by the gods of this mountain
who find it in themselves to forgive everything.
I think I'm saved because I came seeking
what cried out, aching to be sought.
What good it does, this seeking and finding, I cannot tell.
Evil follows like a bad dog yapping
the whole way to the car.
I drive my fist into the hill until it answers.
Child, the flame stream of the west wind says.
Child, say the huddle of out-gloried stars.

The soul may be compared to a sleeper on a golden hill
who even in dreams takes someone, lovelily, to task.
The dark shape of the vulture understands
the road my thought takes.
The flicker trying one spot and then another
has watched me for clues how to proceed.
One is not proud of whom one has led
possibly astray. One understands.
All leaders have meant glory and all ways went astray,
and the moon comes new above the hill.

The wind and the braced light bend to my lips
as if they expected me to tell a secret
kept from them in splendor,
As if they expected me to breathe out—
nectared and mysterious—
the air of other worlds than this.

Watch, sky says as it folds around.
Listen, wind whispers to the shaken gold,
all bent above my throat,
as if some god were answering in his sleep.

Afterword

One of many reasons to admire W. B. Yeats is that his publishing history kept good pace with his writing, so that the reader might follow the development of his technique and ideas from youth into considerable old age. Perhaps that's not the way things work now; at least it's not the way things worked for me, so a book, when it sees the light of day, is likely to be a crazy quilt of different times and dispensations, gathered together at some late moment with the hope that there might be, at least, thematic unity. Some of these poems were written thirty years ago, others after the book was accepted for publication and certain pieces needed replacement or reworking. Things that seem like contradictions might just be one authentic voice speaking at widely divided points in time. That's my plea, anyway. Hale Chatfield was a professor at Hiram College who was the first professional ever to look at my work, which he did with kindness, forbearance, and acuity whose voice I still hear in the hours of revision.

About the Author

David Brendan Hopes' first book of poetry, *The Glacier's Daughters* (U. Mass), won the Juniper Prize and the Saxifrage Prize in 1980. He has since published five volumes of poetry, most recently *Peniel* with St. Julian's Press. He is a successful playwright, with production, at one point of another, in many major American cities, such as New York, Los Angeles, Chicago, Houston, Seattle. In the last three years he has published three novels. The first, *The Falls of the Wyona,* won Red Hen Press' Quill Prize. The second, *Night Sleep, and the Dreams of Lovers,* chronicles the Asheville underground art scene at is was in the 90's the third; *The One with the Beautiful Necklaces,* from Moonshine Cove Press, is a Appalachian family history with a large dose of Mountain Magical Realism.

www.ingramcontent.com/pod-product-compliance
Lightning Source LLC
LaVergne TN
LVHW050938080826
845145LV00004B/1317
9781639800834